Contents

Introduction

Equipment you will need

The process

General Tips

Quick guides to making generic wines

75 Wines recipes in alphabetical order

Introduction

I wanted to share with you the hours of fun that I have had making wine and to let you know how simple the process can be. I'm not going to baffle you with science, but help you experiment and find the rewards in your new hobby.

The satisfaction you get and the sense of achievement that you will experience when all your hard work comes together is amazing. We modestly sip our master piece and say to ourselves "that's not too bad" when really the satisfaction we feel inside screams for recognition. We want to shout "wow that's damn good" and lavish ourselves with praise. Then the dilemma, should we share with our friends to raptures of applause to bolster our pride or just savour our hard earned nectar in solitary self-indulgence.

It doesn't take much to become hooked on making your own wine. After your first success, you will appreciate the process and become an expert in your own field of preference. You may become fanatical about fruit, bonkers about berries or just passionate about potatoes. You will amaze yourself how creative you can become.

I can't take credit for your successes or be liable for your failures, but merely help you to have fun in your chosen hobby. I must advise you to drink responsibly and treat this information with the respect it deserves. In essence this hobby is about having fun, enjoying the process as much as enjoying the wine.

Home-made wine can be made from most vegetable, fruit or grain base. I've made it from cans of fruit syrup and blackcurrant squash, so let your imagination run wild on the possibilities available. There are some great starter kits available which include fruit concentrates, but walking along the hedgerows to collect some berries, is part of the fun for me.

I have made most combinations of flavours, so don't be frightened to experiment. The worse that can happen is that it doesn't suit your taste. You can either mix it with another drink when you serve it or just give it to someone you don't like. You'll be able to watch their expression when they drink it and see how polite they are about your offering.

Once you have made a few different wines, you'll be able to decide your preference. Strangely flavours don't always turn out as expected. Orange wine can come out quite dry, whereas lemon wine can be quite sweet. This can be quite useful to remember when you start to mix and blend ingredients.

I've had some of the best successes with tea. It's very versatile with its variety of different flavours and good to mix. Citrus fruits give a clean, crisp flavour and more depth can be gained by adding spices such as ginger and cloves.

The more you experiment, the more creative you will become. Although I'll give you a list of recipes I encourage you to make up your own as you gain confidence.

To get started this is a list of equipment you will need.

1 x Fermenting Bucket

1x Filtering / Straining Net

2x Gallon Demi Johns

1x Cork / Airlock

1x Syphon tube

1x Fruit Press (optional)

1x Packet of Wine Fining

1x Packet of Wine Yeast

1x Packet Sterilising Solution

1x Demi John Rubber Stopper

6x Wine Bottles

6x Wine Bottle Corks

1x Wine Bottle Corker

1x Wine Filter Kit (optional)

1x Funnel

1x Wine Glass (2x if you want to share)

Cleanliness is very important for all equipment, especially when you first buy them. Make sure that all new items are cleaned with hot water and sterilising solution to ensure all dirt, dust and germs are removed. Once you are happy, then don't get too obsessed with it, as long as you keep on top of it.

My granddad used to make wine in an old tin bath tub. He would chop up some apples, sprinkle on the sugar then top up with water. He would float a piece of toast on the top coated with the yeast he would use. He would cover the tub with a muslin cloth and leave the yeast to ferment the sugar into alcohol.

He would leave the mixture in an outbuilding for several weeks.

He would stir it occasional and pick out the dead wasps which had been enticed under the muslin by the musky aroma. His scientific method for checking the progress of the wine was to scoop up a cup full from time to time. He would often come out of the outbuilding with a smile and glazed eyes, but bless him his wine was great. Eventually it would be ready for others to try but in his words "the wine will evaporate during the brewing process", I guess the sampling had something to do with that.

So just to recap on what I said earlier, don't get too serious about the hobby that will come later if you get competitive. I loved blending recipes to make the perfect wine and entered several in competitions, but I never lost the fun from the process.

Generally we believe that wine comes from crushing fine grapes under our feet in a large vat, but home-made wine is a more organic than that. We can use everyday items that can be purchased from a super market, dug out of the garden or picked from a hedgerow. We can improvise and substitute to create a wide variety of flavours to suit our individual palates.

I've made wine from soaking flower petals, pressing fruit and boiling vegetables. I've used the dry leaves off an oak tree and barley from a farm. I've blended spices such as cloves and ginger to enhance the flavours.

My favourite so far has been Tea and Barley. It is smooth and mellow with a slight whisky taste … umm lovely!!

Although I'll go through each recipe individually, I'd like to explain some of the stages and why they are important.

Once you understand the process it'll give you the confidence to experiment with the ingredients and customise to suit your taste buds.

The only caution I would offer when drinking home-made wine is that it may be stronger in alcohol than you are used to. Also the flavours can sometimes taste like soft drink and it can take you unaware.

Please treat this as a hobby, striving for the best taste you can make, rather than a cheaper alternative to the supermarket. The fun is in the making and the satisfaction of the result.

The Process

The fermentation bucket allows the yeast to attack the fruit / vegetable / grain etc. in its natural state. For example an apple skin would create a barrier for the yeast, so chopping up the apple will allow the yeast to release the juices from the fruit. If you prefer, you could press the apples to release as much juice as possible and add to the flavours.

Some items are harder and may need cooking first. For example a potato may resist the yeast from releasing its contents so easily, so cooking to soften it may help. I'm not a fan of cooking the contents of the recipe because it can create something in the process called Pectin, which can make the wine cloudy. You can buy Pectin Enzymes to overcome this but I prefer not to add anything that I don't need to.

Ingredients such as rice and grain tend to release starch when boiled so I prefer to wash and soaked them in the fermentation bucket with cold water.

Sultanas and raisins help give the wine body and certainly helps root and grain based wines. These added in the fermentation stage will encourage the yeast to work on the main ingredients also.

All contents in the fermentation bucket have to be strained and filter to leave just the liquid which will turn into wine. Don't over force the contents through the net as this will cloud the wine and create more sediment (lees).

The Demi-John is a glass jar that the liquid contents are placed into. Fill the jar up to approximately one inch from the neck. If you need to add a little more water to top it up, do so. Plug the neck with an airlock cork and an airlock filled halfway with water. You will see the gases within the jar start to plop through the water in the airlock. This may be quite rapid to begin with but over time it will slow down.

The jar needs to be stored in a warm place away from direct sunlight. The warmth will allow the yeast to feed off the sugar. Too cold and it won't work, too hot and it will die. Sunlight can take away the colour in the wine therefore cover the jar with brown paper if red wine is exposed to a lot of light. The process can take anything from a few weeks to a few months depending on the temperature and sugar content. The process stops when the yeast has no more sugar to feed on and no more bubbles go through the airlock. Don't be too hasty, sometimes the bubbles can stop if the temperature drops but will start again on its own accord. If it hasn't completed the process it may tasted a little yeasty.

Syphon the contents from one Demi-John to another, carefully avoiding the sediment at the bottom of the jar.

This is the start of the clearing process. Add to the Demi-John either wine finings or a Camden tablet and cork it again with an airlock. Leave the jar in a cool place undisturbed for a week. Repeat the process of syphoning the contents into another Demi-John. Again be careful to avoid the sediment at the bottom of the jar.

At this stage look at how clear the wine is. If it is still cloudy you can either repeat the process of leaving the contents for a week with more wine finings or use my preferred method of using a filtering kit. The clearer the wine, the crisper the taste will be.

When you are happy that it is clear enough plug the jar with a fixed cork and store in a cool dark place.

The wine will mellow over a period of time. The old wives tale about wine getting stronger the longer you leave it, is not true. Although chemical reactions take place after the wine has finished working, this will only mellow and mature the wine, not increase its alcohol content. With most wines, leaving them to stand for a few months will improve their flavour. Unfortunately leaving it too long can have an adverse effect and make them a little bitter. I prefer to store the wine in the Demi-

John so I can periodically try them before I bottle the wine. Sometimes a freshly fermented wine can taste below standard, but generally improves over time. Just bottle it when you are happy.

General tips

Just as a word of warning, never put yeast into a mixture that is too hot or you may kill off the yeast and it'll never work. Always allow the contents of your fermentation bucket to cool to lukewarm or below before stirring in a teaspoon full of brewing yeast. You will see within a day or so the bubbles rising in the bucket and starting to breakdown the fruit, vegetables etc. that you have used.

I have found that freezing some fruits and vegetables can be as effective as cooking to breakdown the item. For example rhubarb when frozen and thawed, will allow you to easily squeeze out the liquid. With carrots they will soften sufficiently to allow the yeast to work on them, without the need to boil.

Wherever possible limit the amount of hot or boiling water to be introduced to the fruit of vegetables. Although sometimes this is unavoidable, the more you cook the ingredients, the more chance you have of creating Pectin which will make the wine cloudy. If the wine becomes too cloudy. Pectin Enzymes can help to overcome this problem. I prefer to use a prevention rather than cure approach, so I can keep the wine as natural as possible.

Temperature is important in the fermenting process. Keep wine at room temperature wherever possible. This will help the yeast to work at a steady rate. Too hot and it may work too aggressively, too cool and it will stop working. If your wine stops for no apparent reason, you can encourage in to start again by placing the demi-john in a sink of warm water until the bubble start to go through the air lock once more.

There is no rule how long a wine takes to complete the fermentation process, this can be from as little as a couple of weeks to a couple of months. You can't rush it, just leave it to run its course. If you filter the wine before it's ready, it may taste yeasty. If you leave the wine to settle on the sludge (lees) on the bottom of the demi-john for too long it can make the wine slightly bitter. I would recommend syphoning the wine off the lees into another demi-john within a few days of when you are sure the process has stopped.

All wines must have acidity of some sort, otherwise fermentation maybe poor and the wine may either taste medicinal or insipid. Citric Acid can be a substitute for Citric Fruit but using lemons and oranges will give additional flavours.

Tannin comes from the skins and stems of red fruit. Also it comes from some tree barks and leaves such as tea. This gives zest to the wine, giving the impression of dryness in the mouth. This is best added to flower, root and grain wines. Too much will cause bitterness, so don't over soak or squeeze fruit. If finished wine is too harsh add a little sugar.

Sugar quantities will affect the sweetness and alcohol content of the wine. As a rule of thumb

2.5 lb of sugar = Dry Wine
3.0 lb of sugar = Medium Wine
3.5 lb of sugar = Sweet Wine

Please remember to take into account the sweetness of the fruit being used. Adding more sugar will not general make the wine have a higher alcohol content.

Extras that can be used to enhance the flavour of the wine, especially if the ingredients tend to be a little bland

Ginger   Malt   Cloves   Vanilla

Brown Sugar   Demerara Sugar

Various Yeasts (Bordeaux, Burgandy etc.)

Quick Guides to making wines

Generic - Grain

1 lb	Grain
3 lb	Sugar
1	Lemon
1	Orange
1 lb	Raisins
1 pint	Tea
	Yeast

Wash grain under hot water then place in the bucket, add sugar and pour over 8 pints of boiling water. When cool add tea, citrus juice, raisins and yeast. Leave in bucket for seven days stirring daily. Strain into Demi-John and leave to work out. Syphon, filter and store for approximately one year.

Generic -Tree Fruit

4lb-6lb Fruit
3lb   Sugar
2   Citrus Fruits or Citric Acid
1   Cup of Tea or Tannin
1 lb Raisins
      Yeast
      Pectin Enzymes   (if hot water used)

Either liquidise or chop fruit. Place fruit in bucket and add 7 pints of cold water. Dissolve sugar in 1 pint of boiling water and add to bucket. Add citrus juice, tea, raisins and yeast. Leave in bucket for seven days stirring daily. Strain into Demi-John and leave to work out. Syphon, filter and store for a few months.

Generic - Root Vegetables

4lb Vegetables
3lb Sugar
3   Citrus Fruits or Citric Acid
1   Cup of tea or Tannin
1 lb Raisins
     Yeast
     Pectin Enzymes   (if hot water used)

Boil vegetables until tender, but don't over boil or wine may become cloudy. Strain water only into bucket and add sugar. When cool add citrus juice, tea and raisins. When cool add yeast. Leave in bucket for seven days stirring daily. Strain into Demi-John and leave to work out. Syphon, filter and store for approximately one year.

Generic - Leaves and Flowers

4-6 pints of Flower Petals or Leaves
3lb Sugar
2 Citrus Fruits or Citric Acid
1pint Tea or Tannin
1lb Raisins
    Yeast

Place flowers / leaves in bucket and pour over 8 pints of boiling water, add sugar and leave to cool. Add citrus juice, tea, raisins and yeast. Leave in bucket for seven days stirring daily. Strain into Demi-John and leave to work out. Syphon, filter and store for a few months.

Generic - Berries

3lb-4lb Berries
3lb Sugar
2   Citrus Fruits or Citric Acid   (optional)
1lb Raisins   (optional)
       Yeast

Chop, prick or mash Berries as appropriate. Pour over hot water (depending on fruit) add sugar and stir well. When cool add yeast and any other ingredients you require. Leave in bucket for seven days stirring daily. Strain into Demi-John and leave to work out. Syphon, filter and store for a few months.

Generic - Citrus Fruits

6-12 Pieces of fruit (depending on size)
3lb Sugar
     Yeast

Grate peel (no pith) into bucket, add sugar and pour 8 pints of boiling water. When cool add citrus juice and yeast. Leave in bucket for seven days stirring daily. Strain into Demi-John and leave to work out. Syphon, filter and store for a few months.

I hope so far, that I have wetted your appetite and sparked your imagination to dive into the wonderful combination of flavours waiting for you.

You are not looking to copy your favourite label or replicate a well-known brand. My understanding of making your own wine is about finding your new creation.

I can remember how proud my dad was when he sampled his wine. He would never wait for it to mature he would dive in as soon as the airlock lay still. It was only a taster, but then a couple of weeks later another little taster and so on. When it was ready half a bottle was missing. Mum would tease him but always find him another recipe to make.

I can remember them making wine for years. Mum was a country girl and knew every berry in the hedgerow. She was the font of all knowledge and very resourceful. I can remember her bringing home a large tin of orange puree which was meant for making marmalade. Yes the ingredients of another wine making triumph.

So I guess I'm the third generation of wine maker in my family and I'm sure it goes back further than that. People that lived off the land understood what the land had to offer and didn't waste anything.

I've now listed wines that I've created over the years and most came from my imagination. I haven't bored you with the ones that went wrong but I have given you the best of the best that I've made.

Apple and Cloves

10lb Apples
3lb Demerara Sugar
3lb White Sugar
2   Lemons
10   Cloves
2lb Sultanas
     Yeast   (enough for 2 gallons)

Dissolve the sugar in a bucket with two gallons of boiling water. Add cloves and juice for lemons. When cool add chopped apples, sultanas and yeast. Leave in bucket stirring daily for 7 days. Strain into demi-johns and follow fermenting process.

Very nice!! Smooth medium wine with tangy taste, similar to cider

Apple and Grapefruit

3lb Apples
3   Grapefruits
3lb Sugar
1lb Raisins
    Yeast

Dissolve sugar in a bucket with 8 pints of boiling water. When cool add the juice from the grapefruits and add chopped apples, raisins and yeast. . Leave in bucket stirring daily for 7 days. Strain into demi-john and follow fermenting process.

Light medium dry wine, great with a meal

Apple and Plum

2lb Apples
2lb Plums
3lb Sugar
2   Lemons
    Yeast

Stone and chop plums. Core and chop apples. Place in bucket with sugar, lemon juice and 8 pints of warm water. When cool enough add yeast. Leave in bucket stirring daily for 7 days. Strain into demi-john and follow fermenting process.

Nice medium fruity wine, ready to drink anytime

Apricot

1lb Dried Apricots
1lb Demerara Sugar
2lb White Sugar
    Yeast

Dissolve sugar in 8 pints of boiling water. When cool enough added finely chopped apricots and yeast. Leave in bucket stirring daily for 7 days. Strain into demi-john and follow fermenting process.

Dry and smooth, went down a treat

Beetroot and Barley

5lb Beetroot
½lb Barley
3lb Sugar
1oz Ginger
2 Lemons
   Yeast

Slice beetroot and boil until just tender. Wash barley with hot wash and place in bucket with finely chopped ginger and sugar. Pour over water from beetroots and top up to 8 pints. When cool add juice from lemons and yeast. Leave in bucket stirring daily for 7 days. Strain into demi-john and follow fermenting process.

Light dry and crisp, perfect with a meal

Beetroot and Cloves

5lb Beetroot
½lb Sultanas
3lb Sugar
2 Lemons
6 Cloves
　 Yeast

Slice beetroot and boil until just tender.
Place sugar in bucket and pour over water from beetroots. When cool enough add sultanas, lemon juice, cloves and yeast. Leave in bucket stirring daily for 7 days. Strain into demi-john and follow fermenting process.

Very nice!! Smooth medium / dry wine.

Berries (mixed)

4lb   Elderberries
1½lb Blackberries
1lb   Sloes
6lb   Sugar
        Yeast   (enough for 2 gallons)

Put all berries into bucket with sugar and pour over 2 gallons of boiling water. Allow sugar to dissolve and when cool enough add yeast. Leave in bucket stirring daily for 7 days. Don't over squeeze when straining into demi-johns and follow fermenting process.

Very nice!! Fruity medium wine, as good as any I've bought in a shop

Blackberry

3lb Blackberries
3lb Sugar
    Yeast

Put blackberries into bucket with sugar and pour over 8 pints of boiling water. Allow sugar to dissolve and when cool enough add yeast. Leave in bucket stirring daily for 7 days. Don't over squeeze when straining into demi-john and follow fermenting process.

Bloody handsome!! Light fruity medium dry wine

Blackberry and Apple

3lb Blackberries
5lb Apples
5lb Sugar
1lb Raisins
   Yeast   (enough for 2 gallons)

Place blackberries and sugar in bucket and pour over 8 pints of boiling water. Top with 8 pints of cold water. Add chopped apple and raisins and when cool enough add yeast. Leave in bucket stirring daily for 7 days. Strain into demi-john and follow fermenting process.

Very nice!! Dry crisp and fruity

Blood Orange

3lb (12) Blood Oranges
3lb   Sugar
       Yeast

Grate peel (no pith) into bucket with the sugar. Pour over 8 pints of boiling water to dissolve. Add orange juice. When cool enough add yeast. . Leave in bucket stirring daily for 7 days. Strain into demi-john and follow fermenting process.

Really nice!! Smooth and very drinkable

Blood Orange and Date

3lb (12) Blood Oranges
1lb   Dried Dates
½lb   Sultanas
5lb   Sugar
          Yeast   (enough for 2 gallons)

Grate peel (no pith) into bucket with the sugar. Pour over 8 pints of boiling water to dissolve. Add 8 pints cold water and orange juice. When cool enough add finely chopped dates, sultanas and yeast. Leave in bucket stirring daily for 7 days. Strain into demi-johns and follow fermenting process.

Dry with a bit of a kick, lovely with food

Carrot and Ginger

3lb Carrots
3lb Sugar
1lb Sultanas
2oz Ginger
2   Lemons
     Yeast

Slice and boil carrots until tender. Peel and slice ginger into bucket with sugar, sultanas and lemon juice. Pour over water from carrots and top up to 8pints. When cool enough add yeast. Leave in bucket stirring daily for 7 days. Strain into demi-john and follow fermenting process.

Dry but warming, great for a winter treat

Carrot and Potato

2lb Carrots
2lb Potatoes
3lb Sugar
½lb Sultanas
½ Pint of tea
2 Lemons
　 Yeast

Boil carrots and potatoes until tender. Pour water from vegetables and tea into bucket and top up to 8 pints. Add sugar sultanas and lemon juice. When cool enough add yeast. Leave in bucket stirring daily for 7 days. Strain into demi-john and follow fermenting process.

Rather nice!! Dry and crisp great with food

Cherry

4lb Cherries
3lb Sugar
    Yeast

Cut cherries in half and stone. Place them in a bucket with the sugar. Pour over 8 pints of boiling water. When cool enough add yeast. Leave in bucket stirring daily for 7 days. Don't over squeeze when straining into demi-john and follow fermenting process.

Fruity but dry, complements tangy desserts

Citrus Cocktail

3   Oranges
3   Grapefruits
3   Limes
3   Lemons
3lb Sugar
    Yeast

Grate peel (no pith) from fruit into bucket. Add fruit juices and top up to 8 pints with cold water. Add sugar and yeast, stir well until dissolved. Leave in bucket stirring daily for 7 days. Strain into demi-john and follow fermenting process.

Rather good!! Very smooth medium wine

Crab Apple

6lb Crab Apples
1lb Sultanas
3lb Sugar
2 Lemons
　 Yeast

Place crab apples (whole) into bucket with sultanas, sugar and lemon juice. Pour over 8 pints of boiling water. Stir well to dissolve sugar. When cool enough add yeast. Leave in bucket stirring daily for 7 days. Strain into demi-john and follow fermenting process.

Nice pleasant dry wine

Currant

2lb Currants
3lb Sugar
2   Lemons
       Yeast

Place sugar and lemon juice in bucket and pour over 3 pints boiling water. When sugar dissolved top up with 5 pints cold water. When cool enough add currants and yeast. Leave in bucket stirring daily for 7 days. Strain into demi-john and follow fermenting process.

Lovely wine!! Quite sweet but very smooth

Date

1lb Dried Dates
1lb Sultanas
3lb Sugar
2   Lemons
     Yeast

Place sugar and lemon juice in bucket and pour over 3 pints boiling water. When sugar dissolved top up with 5 pints cold water. When cool enough add sultanas, finely chopped dates and yeast. Leave in bucket stirring daily for 7 days. Strain into demi-john and follow fermenting process.

Bloody handsome!! Fairly dry but very smooth

Date and Lime Cordial

1   Bottle Rose's Lime Cordial
3lb   Sugar
½lb   Dried Dates
½lb   Raisins
       Yeast

Place sugar in bucket and pour over 3 pints boiling water. When sugar dissolved add lime cordial and 4 pints of cold water. When cool enough add raisins, finely chopped dates and yeast. Leave in bucket stirring daily for 7 days. Strain into demi-john and follow fermenting process.

Rather nice!! Very smooth slightly tart taste

Date and Rice

½lb Dried Dates
1lb Rice
½lb Sultanas
3lb Sugar
2 Lemons
    Yeast

Place sugar in bucket and pour over 3 pints boiling water. When sugar dissolved add further 5 pints of cold water. Wash rice in cold water to remove starch then add to bucket with finely chopped dates, sultanas and lemon juice. When cool enough add yeast. Leave in bucket stirring daily for 7 days. Strain into demi-john and follow fermenting process.

Smooth medium everyday wine

Earl Grey Tea

16 Earl Grey Tea Bags
2lb White Sugar
1lb Demerara Sugar
1lb Sultanas
2 Lemons
   Yeast

Place tea bags in bucket and pour over 8 pints of boiling water, stir well. After 10 minutes take out tea bags and add sugar to dissolve. When cool enough add sultanas, lemon juice and yeast. Leave in bucket stirring daily for 7 days. Strain into demi-john and follow fermenting process.

Really smooth medium dry wine

Elderberry

3lb Elderberries
3lb Sugar
    Yeast

Remove berries from stork with a fork. Wash them thoroughly with cold water. Place berries and sugar in bucket and pour over 8 pints of boiling water. When cool enough add yeast. Leave in bucket stirring daily for 7 days. Don't over squeeze when straining into demi-john and follow fermenting process.

Very nice!! As good as any dry red wine you would buy

Elderberry and Apple

2lb   Elderberries
2lb   Apples
2lb   White Sugar
1lb   Brown Sugar
      Yeast

Remove berries from stork with a fork. Wash them thoroughly with cold water. Place berries and sugar in bucket and pour over 8 pints of boiling water. When cool enough add chopped apples and yeast. Leave in bucket stirring daily for 7 days. Don't over squeeze when straining into demi-john and follow fermenting process.

Smooth dry and fruity with a crisp taste

Elderberry and Blackberry

3lb Elderberries
3lb Blackberries
6lb Sugar
    Yeast   (enough for 2 gallons)

Remove elderberries from stork with a fork. Wash them thoroughly with cold water. Place all berries and sugar in bucket and pour over 2 gallons of boiling water. When cool enough add yeast. Leave in bucket stirring daily for 7 days. Don't over squeeze when straining into demi-johns and follow fermenting process.

Great wine!! Medium fruity, full bodied. As good as any red wine you would buy

Elderberry and Grape

3lb Home Grown Grapes
2lb Elderberries
3lb Sugar
2   Lemons
     Yeast

Remove berries from stork with a fork. Wash them thoroughly with cold water. Place berries and sugar in bucket and pour over 8 pints of boiling water. When cool enough add lemon juice, grapes and yeast. Leave in bucket stirring daily for 7 days. Don't over squeeze when straining into demi-john and follow fermenting process.

Smooth dry and fruity with a crisp taste

Elderberry and Orange

3lb Elderberries
7 Oranges
3lb Sugar
    Yeast

Remove berries from stork with a fork. Wash them thoroughly with cold water. Place berries, grated orange peel (no pith) and sugar in bucket and pour over 8 pints of boiling water. When cool enough add orange juice and yeast. Leave in bucket stirring daily for 7 days. Don't over squeeze when straining into demi-john and follow fermenting process.

Quite dry and fruity

Elderflower

1   Pint Elder Flowers
3lb Sugar
½lb Sultanas
½   Pint of Cold Tea
2   Lemons
    Yeast

Cut flower heads from stalks to make up a pint of flower head. Place flowers and sugar in bucket and pour over 8 pints of boiling water. When cool enough add tea, sultanas, lemon juice and yeast. Leave in bucket stirring daily for 7 days. Strain into demi-john and follow fermenting process.

Quite a perfume taste but very refreshing

Fig

1lb Dried Figs
½lb Sultanas
3lb Sugar
    Yeast

Place sugar in bucket and pour over 8 pints of boiling water. When cool enough add finely chopped figs, sultanas and yeast. Leave in bucket stirring daily for 7 days. Strain into demi-john and follow fermenting process.

Great success!! Tastes like a liqueur, very smooth and dry

Gooseberry

3lb Gooseberries
½lb Sultanas
3lb Sugar
    Yeast

Cut gooseberries in half and place in bucket with sugar and sultanas. Pour over 8 pints of boiling water and stir until sugar dissolved. When cool enough add yeast. Leave in bucket stirring daily for 7 days. Strain into demi-john and follow fermenting process.

Excellent!! Medium, smooth and very drinkable

Gooseberry and Apple

2lb Gooseberries
2lb Apples
1½lb Demerara Sugar
1½lb White Sugar
½lb Raisins
2 Lemons
    Yeast

Cut gooseberries in half and place in bucket with chopped apples, sugar, lemon juice and raisins. Pour over 8 pints of boiling water and stir until sugar dissolved. When cool enough add yeast. Leave in bucket stirring daily for 7 days. Strain into demi-john and follow fermenting process.

Lovely wine!! Crisp and dry

Grape

3lb Grapes (either white or black)
3lb Sugar
     Yeast

Place grapes in bucket and mash to break skins. Cover with sugar and pour over 8 pints of boiling water. When cool enough add yeast. Leave in bucket stirring daily for 7 days. Strain into demi-john and follow fermenting process.

Pleasant crisp / dry wine

Flavours will vary with type of grape and whether you mix sugars etc.

Grape and Lime Cordial

3lb Grapes (either white or black)
½   Bottle Rose's Lime Cordial
3lb Sugar
     Yeast

Place grapes in bucket and mash to break skins. Cover with sugar and pour over 7 pints of boiling water. When cool enough add cordial and yeast. Leave in bucket stirring daily for 7 days. Strain into demi-john and follow fermenting process.

Very nice!! Crisp / dry wine with a tangy twist

Grapefruit and Ginger

5 Grapefruits
2oz Root Ginger
1½lb Demerara Sugar
1½lb White Sugar
  Yeast

Finely chop and bruise ginger. Grate peel of grapefruit (no pith) and place in bucket with sugar and ginger. Pour over 7 points of boiling water, stir to dissolve. When cool enough add grapefruit juice and yeast. Leave in bucket stirring daily for 7 days. Strain into demi-john and follow fermenting process.

Nice smooth wine with a slight bitter after taste

Haw

4lb Haws
3lb Sugar
    Yeast

Pick ripe berries from a hawthorn bush and wash thoroughly. Place berries in bucket with sugar and pour over 8 pints of boiling water. Stir well until sugar dissolved. When cool enough add yeast. Leave in bucket stirring daily for 7 days. Strain into demi-john and follow fermenting process.

Very subtle wine without a strong taste

Kiwi

12　Kiwis
1lb　Sultanas
3lb　Sugar
2　　Lemons
　　　Yeast

Place sugar in bucket and pour over 8 pints of water to dissolve. Peel and chop kiwis, then add them to the bucket with sultanas and lemon juice. When cool enough add yeast. Leave in bucket stirring daily for 7 days. Strain into demi-john and follow fermenting process.

Quite a light pleasant wine with a subtle dryness

Kiwi and Lime Cordial

12 Kiwis
½ Bottle of Rose's Lime Cordial
3lb Sugar
1lb Raisins
   Yeast

Place sugar in bucket and pour over 7½ pints of water to dissolve. Peel and chop kiwis, then add them to the bucket with raisins and lime cordial. When cool enough add yeast. Leave in bucket stirring daily for 7 days. Strain into demi-john and follow fermenting process.

Very good!! Medium sweet and very drinkable

Kiwi and Grapefruit

10 Kiwis
2 Grapefruits
3lb Sugar
½lb Sultanas
  Yeast

Grate peel from grapefruits (no pith) and add to bucket with sugar. Pour over 8 pints of boiling water to dissolve. When cool enough peel and chop kiwis, add them to bucket with sultanas and yeast. . Leave in bucket stirring daily for 7 days. Strain into demi-john and follow fermenting process.

Pleasant wine, light and fairly dry

Lemon

6   Lemons
3lb Sugar
    Yeast

Grate peel from lemons (no pith) and add to bucket with sugar. Pour over 8 pints of boiling water to dissolve. When cool enough add lemon juice and yeast. . Leave in bucket stirring daily for 7 days. Strain into demi-john and follow fermenting process.

Lovely refreshing taste!! Medium sweet and quite smooth

Lemon and Barley

4   Lemons
1lb Barley
3lb Sugar
    Yeast

Wash barley in boiling water, rinse and place in bucket. Grate peel (no pith) of lemons, add to bucket with sugar. Pour over 8 pints of boiling water and leave to dissolve sugar. When cool enough add lemon juice and yeast. . Leave in bucket stirring daily for 7 days. Strain into demi-john and follow fermenting process.

Lovely wine!! Medium sweet with a slight spirit taste from the barley

Lemon and Lime

4   Lemons
4   Limes
3lb Sugar
    Yeast

Grate peel (no pith) of lemons and limes, add to bucket with sugar. Pour over 8 pints of boiling water and leave to dissolve sugar. When cool enough add lemon and lime juice and yeast. . Leave in bucket stirring daily for 7 days. Strain into demi-john and follow fermenting process.

Quite sweet but very smooth, great chilled on a summer's day

Lime Cordial and Barley

½ Bottle of Rose's Lime Cordial
1lb Barley
1lb Sultanas
3lb Sugar
    Yeast

Wash barley in boiling water, rinse and place in bucket. Add sugar and pour over 7½ pints of boiling water. Leave to dissolve sugar. When cool enough add lime cordial, sultanas and yeast. Leave in bucket stirring daily for 7 days. Strain into demi-john and follow fermenting process.

Very pleasant!! Sweet and tangy

Lime Cordial and Pineapple

2 Pineapples
½ Bottle of Rose's Lime Cordial
½lb Sultanas
3lb Sugar
   Yeast

Peel and chop pineapples. Place in bucket with sugar and pour over 7½ pints of boiling water. When cool enough add lime cordial, sultanas and yeast. Leave in bucket stirring daily for 7 days. Strain into demi-john and follow fermenting process.

Very nice!! Light medium dry wine

Mint

- 1½ Pints of Fresh Garden Mint
- 3lb Sugar
- 2 Lemons
- ½ Pint of Tea
- Yeast

Chop mint (just leaves) and place in bucket with sugar. Pour over 7½ pints of boiling water. When cool enough add cold tea, lemon juice and yeast. Leave in bucket stirring daily for 7 days. Strain into demi-john and follow fermenting process.

Bloody handsome!! Medium, smooth and very drinkable

Oak Leaf

4   Pints of Oak Leaves
1lb Sultanas
3lb Sugar
2   Lemons
    Yeast

Collect oak leaves in the autumn when they have turned brown and fallen to the ground, wash them thoroughly in cool water. Add them to the bucket with the sugar and pour over 8 pints of boiling water. When cool scoop out the leaves leaving just the brown liquid. Add sultanas, lemon juice and yeast. Leave in bucket stirring daily for 7 days. Strain into demi-john and follow fermenting process.

Amazing!! Smooth like a mellow whisky

Orange and Barley

6 Oranges
1lb Barley
3lb Sugar
   Yeast

Wash barley in boiling water, rinse and place in bucket. Grate peel (no pith) of oranges, add to bucket with sugar. Pour over 7½ pints of boiling water and leave to dissolve sugar. When cool enough add orange juice and yeast. Leave in bucket stirring daily for 7 days. Strain into demi-john and follow fermenting process.

Light taste, quite dry but very smooth

Orange and Ginger

8   Oranges
2oz Root Ginger
3lb Sugar
    Yeast

Grate peel (no pith) of oranges, add to bucket with peeled chopped ginger and sugar. Pour over 7½ pints of boiling water and leave to dissolve sugar. When cool enough add orange juice and yeast. Leave in bucket stirring daily for 7 days. Strain into demi-john and follow fermenting process.

Very nice!! Dry, tangy with a warm mellow feel to it

Orange and Lemon

4 Oranges
4 Lemons
3lb Sugar
   Yeast

Grate peel (no pith) of oranges, add to bucket sugar. Pour over 7½ pints of boiling water and leave to dissolve sugar. When cool enough add orange juice and yeast. Leave in bucket stirring daily for 7 days. Strain into demi-john and follow fermenting process.

Very nice!! Crisp, light and dry. Great chilled on a summer's day

Orange and Rice

4 Oranges
1lb Rice
3lb Sugar
1lb Sultanas
   Yeast

Grate peel (no pith) of oranges, add to bucket sugar. Pour over 7½ pints of boiling water and leave to dissolve sugar. When cool enough add orange juice, sultanas and yeast. Wash rice in cold water to remove starch then add to bucket. Leave in bucket stirring daily for 7 days. Strain into demi-john and follow fermenting process.

Very pleasant!! Medium dry and slightly tangy

Parsnip

5lb Parsnips
3lb Sugar
½lb Raisins
2   Lemons
     Yeast

Chop parsnips (including skins) and boil in saucepan until just tender. Add water from pan to bucket and dissolve sugar. Top up to 8 pints with cold water. When cool enough add lemon juice, raisin and yeast. Leave in bucket stirring daily for 7 days. Strain into demi-john and follow fermenting process.

Lovely wine!! Smooth medium and very drinkable

Peach

4lb Peaches (very ripe)
3lb Sugar
　　 Yeast

Remove stones and place fruit in bucket. Squash fruit as much as possible, add sugar and pour over 8 pints of boiling water. When cool enough add yeast. Leave in bucket stirring daily for 7 days. Strain into demi-john and follow fermenting process.

Dry with a light taste, ideal chilled with a meal

Pear and Clove

5lb Pears (very ripe)
3lb Sugar
½lb Sultanas
2 Lemons
10 Cloves
    Yeast

Place sugar in bucket and pour over 8 pints of boiling water. When cool enough add chopped pears, sultanas, cloves, lemon juice and yeast. Leave in bucket stirring daily for 7 days. Strain into demi-john and follow fermenting process.

Really nice!! Smooth and mellow with a spicy twist

Pineapple

3 Pineapples
3lb Sugar
1 Lemon
2 Oranges
  Yeast

Grate peel (no pith) of oranges and lemon, add to bucket sugar. Pour over 7 pints of boiling water and leave to dissolve sugar. When cool enough peel and chop pineapples and add to bucket with orange juice, lemon juice and yeast. Leave in bucket stirring daily for 7 days. Strain into demi-john and follow fermenting process.

Very nice!! Dry and crisp, lovely chilled on a summer's day

Plum

8lb Plums (very ripe)
1lb Sultanas
4   Lemons
5lb Sugar
    Yeast   (enough for 2 gallons)

Dissolve sugar in bucket with boiling water then top up to 2 gallons. When cool enough remove stones from plums and add them to bucket with sultanas, lemon juice and yeast. Leave in bucket stirring daily for 7 days. Strain into demi-john and follow fermenting process.

One of my favourites!! Smooth medium wine that brings you back for more

Plum and Clove

4lb Plums (very ripe)
½lb Sultanas
3lb Sugar
20 Cloves
    Yeast

Dissolve sugar in bucket with 8 pints of boiling water. When cool enough remove stones from plums and add them to bucket with sultanas, cloves and yeast. Leave in bucket stirring daily for 7 days. Strain into demi-john and follow fermenting process.

Lovely wine!! Smooth medium with a spicy twist

Potato

5lb Potatoes
3lb Sugar
½lb Raisins
2   Lemons
     Yeast

Chop potatoes (including skins) and boil in saucepan until just tender. Add water from pan to bucket and dissolve sugar. Top up to 8 pints with cold water. When cool enough add lemon juice, raisin and yeast. Leave in bucket stirring daily for 7 days. Strain into demi-john and follow fermenting process.

Wow!! Dry smooth, one of the best wines I have made, as good as any you could buy

Rice

1lb Rice
1lb Sultanas
3lb Sugar
2 Lemons
   Yeast

Place sugar in bucket and dissolve with 8 pints of boiling water. Wash rice in cold water to remove starch and when cool enough add to bucket with sultanas, lemon juice and yeast. Leave in bucket stirring daily for 7 days. Strain into demi-john and follow fermenting process.

Very nice indeed!! Dry crisp, great chilled with a meal

Rice (spiced version)

1lb Rice
1lb Sultanas
3lb Sugar
2 Lemons
1 Cinnamon Stick (approx. ½oz)
8 Cloves
   Yeast

Place sugar in bucket and dissolve with 8 pints of boiling water. Wash rice in cold water to remove starch and when cool enough add to bucket with sultanas, lemon juice and yeast. Leave in bucket stirring daily for 7 days. Strain into demi-john and follow fermenting process.

Very mellow!! Smooth medium wine

Redcurrant

5lb Redcurrant
3lb Sugar
   Yeast

Place redcurrant and sugar in bucket and pour over 2 pints of boiling water. Mash redcurrant then top up with a further 6 pints of cold water. When cool enough add yeast. Leave in bucket stirring daily for 7 days. Strain into demi-john and follow fermenting process.

Very nice!! Dry light and crisp with a fruity taste

Rhubarb

3lb Rhubarb
3lb Sugar
   Yeast

Chop rhubarb and freeze. When you thaw the fruit, it will have soften, allowing you to squeeze out the juice. Place sugar in bucket and dissolve in 2 pints of boiling water. When cool enough add the juice from the rhubarb, yeast and top up to a total of 8 pints with further cold water. Leave in bucket stirring daily for 7 days. Strain into demi-john and follow fermenting process.

Bloody Handsome!! Dry and smooth

Rhubarb and Blackberry

3lb Rhubarb
2lb Blackberries
3lb Sugar
    Yeast

Chop rhubarb and freeze. When you thaw the fruit, it will have soften, allowing you to squeeze out the juice. Place sugar in bucket and dissolve in 2 pints of boiling water. When cool enough add the juice from the rhubarb, blackberries, yeast and top up to a total of 8 pints with further cold water. Leave in bucket stirring daily for 7 days. Strain into demi-john and follow fermenting process.

Wow!! Medium smooth and fruity

Rhubarb and Ginger

3lb Rhubarb
2oz Root Ginger
3lb Sugar
    Yeast

Chop rhubarb and freeze. When you thaw the fruit, it will have soften, allowing you to squeeze out the juice. Place sugar in bucket and dissolve in 2 pints of boiling water. When cool enough add the juice from the rhubarb, peeled chopped ginger, yeast and top up to a total of 8 pints with further cold water. Leave in bucket stirring daily for 7 days. Strain into demi-john and follow fermenting process.

Lovely!! Medium, smooth and warming

Rose Hip

4lb Rose Hips
3lb Sugar
2 Lemons
    Yeast

Place ripe rose hips in bucket with sugar and pour over 8 pints of boiling water. Stir well until sugar dissolved. When cool enough add lemon juice and yeast. Leave in bucket stirring daily for 7 days. Strain into demi-john and follow fermenting process.

Very subtle rosé wine without a strong taste

Rose Petal

4   Pints of Rose Petals
1   Oranges
1   Lemons
3lb Sugar
    Yeast

Place rose petals in bucket with sugar and pour over 8 pints of boiling water. Leave to stand overnight then remove all petals leaving liquid only. Add orange and lemon juice also yeast. Leave in bucket stirring daily for 7 days. Strain into demi-john and follow fermenting process.

Very nice!! Smooth medium rosé wine with subtle flowery taste

Rose Petal (spiced version)

4   Pints of Rose Petals
2   Lemons
3lb Sugar
2oz Root Ginger
1   Cinnamon Stick (approx. ½oz)
    Yeast

Place rose petals in bucket with sugar and pour over 8 pints of boiling water. Leave to stand overnight then remove all petals leaving liquid only. Add lemon juice, cinnamon, peeled chopped ginger and yeast. Leave in bucket stirring daily for 7 days. Strain into demi-john and follow fermenting process.

Lovely!! Smooth medium and warming

Rose Petal and Vanilla

4   Pints of Rose Petals
1   Limes
1   Lemons
3lb Sugar
1   Vanilla Pod
    Yeast

Place rose petals in bucket with sugar and pour over 8 pints of boiling water. Leave to stand overnight then remove all petals leaving liquid only. Add lime and lemon juice, vanilla pod and yeast. Leave in bucket stirring daily for 7 days. Strain into demi-john and follow fermenting process.

Nice and mellow!! Smooth medium rosé

Sloe

4lb Sloes
3lb Sugar
   Yeast

Place sloes and sugar in bucket and pour over 8 pints of boiling water. When cool enough add yeast. Leave in bucket stirring daily for 7 days. Strain into demi-john and follow fermenting process.

Always a favourite!! Nice full bodied red wine with a slightly dry after taste

Strawberry

4lb Strawberries
3lb Sugar
2   Lemons
    Yeast

Chop strawberries and freeze. When you thaw the fruit, it will have soften allow the juice to be released more easily. Place sugar in bucket and pour over 7 pints of boiling water. When cool enough add strawberries, lemon juice and yeast. Leave in bucket stirring daily for 7 days. Strain into demi-john and follow fermenting process.

Very Nice!! Fruity dry rosé

Strawberry and Apple

2lb Strawberries
3lb Apples
½lb Sultanas
3lb Sugar
1 Lemon
    Yeast

Chop strawberries and freeze. When you thaw the fruit, it will have soften allow the juice to be released more easily. Place sugar in bucket and pour over 7 pints of boiling water. When cool enough add strawberries, chopped apples, sultanas, lemon juice and yeast. Leave in bucket stirring daily for 7 days. Strain into demi-john and follow fermenting process.

Drier crisper rosé, lovely chilled with food

Sultana

2lb Sultanas
3lb Sugar
2   Lemons
     Yeast

Place sugar in bucket and pour over 8 pints of boiling water. When cool enough add sultanas, lemon juice and yeast. Leave in bucket stirring daily for 7 days. Strain into demi-john and follow fermenting process.

You'll come back for more!!
Medium sweet, very smooth

Tea

16 Tea Bags
1½lb White Sugar
1½lb Demerara Sugar
½lb Sultanas
2 Lemons
    Yeast

Place tea bags in bucket with sugar, pour over 8 pints of boiling water. Leave for 10 minutes and remove tea bags. When cool enough add sultanas, lemon juice and yeast. Leave in bucket stirring daily for 7 days. Strain into demi-john and follow fermenting process.

Very nice indeed!! Medium dry, very smooth

Tea and Barley

16 Tea Bags
½lb Barley
½lb Sultanas
3lb Sugar
2   Lemons
    Yeast

Place tea bags in bucket with sugar, pour over 8 pints of boiling water. Leave for 10 minutes and remove tea bags. Wash barley in boiling water. When cool enough add barley, sultanas, lemon juice and yeast. Leave in bucket stirring daily for 7 days. Strain into demi-john and follow fermenting process.

My best creation!! Medium sweet and very smooth, one of my nicest tea recipes

Tea and Date

10   Tea Bags
½lb Dried Dates
2½lb Demerara Sugar
2   Lemons
      Yeast

Place tea bags in bucket with sugar, pour over 8 pints of boiling water. Leave for 10 minutes and remove tea bags. When cool enough add chopped dates, lemon juice and yeast. Leave in bucket stirring daily for 7 days. Strain into demi-john and follow fermenting process.

Wow lovely!! Smooth medium wine, taste like a liqueur

Tea and Ginger

10 Tea Bags
2oz Root Ginger
3lb Sugar
1lb Sultanas
2   Lemons
     Yeast

Place tea bags in bucket with sugar, pour over 8 pints of boiling water. Leave for 10 minutes and remove tea bags. When cool enough add peeled chopped ginger, sultanas, lemon juice and yeast. Leave in bucket stirring daily for 7 days. Strain into demi-john and follow fermenting process.

Winter treat!! Nice smooth warming wine

Water Melon and Lemon

1 Large Water Melon
4 Lemons
3lb Sugar
   Yeast

Grate peel (no pith) of lemons in bucket with sugar. Pour over 7 pints of boiling water. When cool enough chop melon into small squares (no skin) and place in bucket. Add lemon juice and yeast. Leave in bucket stirring daily for 7 days. Strain into demi-john and follow fermenting process.

Refreshing!! Very light flavours

Water Melon and Pineapple

1   Large Water Melon
1   Large Pineapple
3lb Sugar
½   Pint of Tea
1   Lemon
    Yeast

Place sugar in bucket and pour over 6 pints of boiling water. When cool enough chop melon and pineapple into squares (no skin) and place in bucket. Add lemon juice and yeast. Leave in bucket stirring daily for 7 days. Strain into demi-john and follow fermenting process.

Pleasant!! Medium and subtle flavours

Printed in Great Britain
by Amazon